Big Sailor

My First Big ABC

Ages 3-5

Vol.9 Y · Z

Peachidu!
Your study buddy

My First Big ABC Book Series
Big Sailor Edu

Copyright © 2021 Cambridge Dynasty Press

For permission requests, bulk order information, or any busine ss related inquiries, please contact the publisher at the email address below.

Cambridge Dynasty Press
30 N Gould St. STE4000
Sheridan, WY 82801
Email: Bestsailoredu@Gmail.com

Written, Designed, and Printed in the United States of America

978-1-955650-01-4(Paperback)

47678459

Hi! Nice to meet you. My name is Peachidu!

I am your study buddy for this book!

1. Building Skills for Pen Control
2. Recognizing Alphabet Letters
3. Building Confidence
4. Enjoying a Good Book
5. Being Patient with Practice
6. Developing Creative Thinking
7. Being Proud of Achievement
8. Having Fun

This book belongs to

_____

(name)

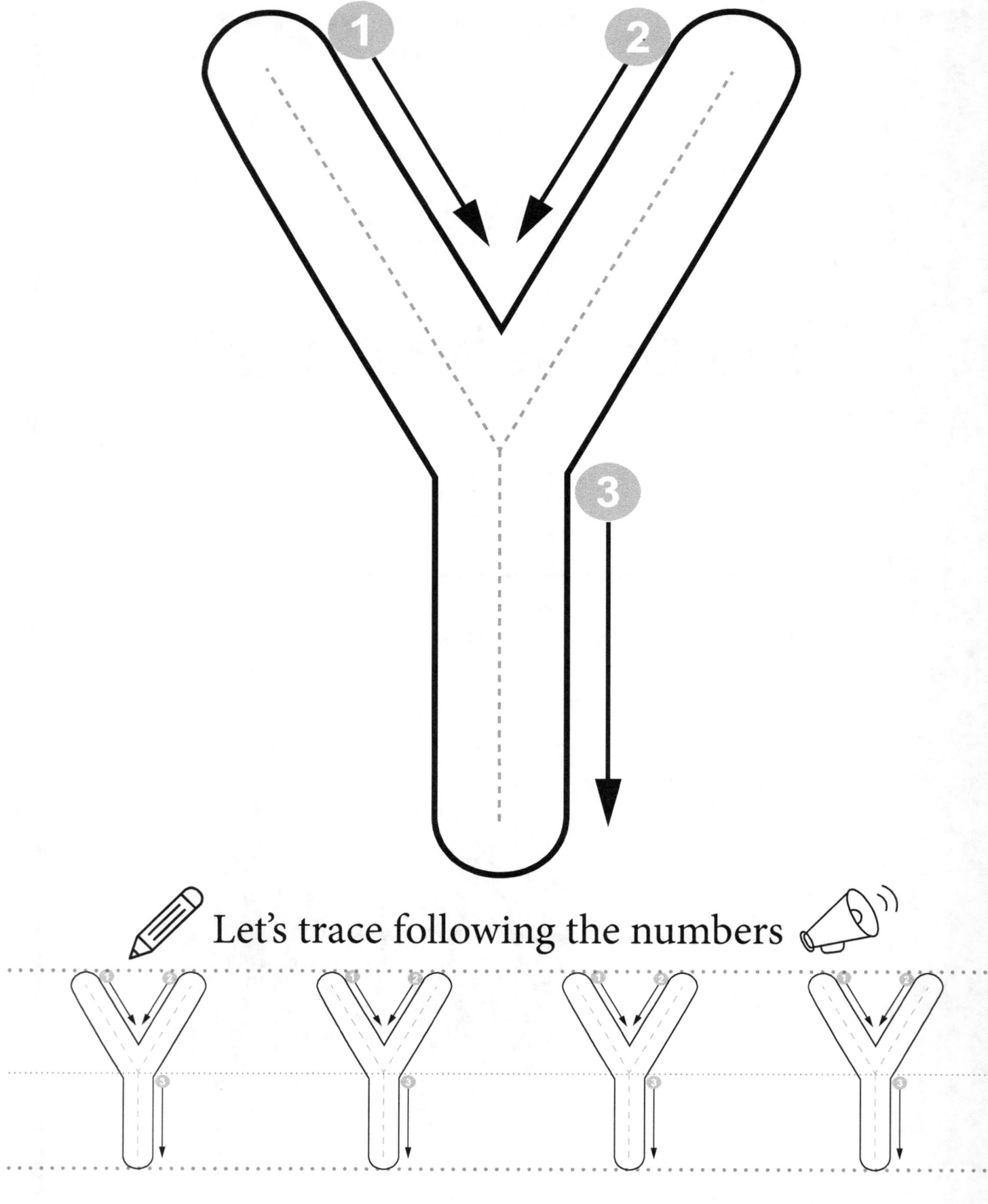

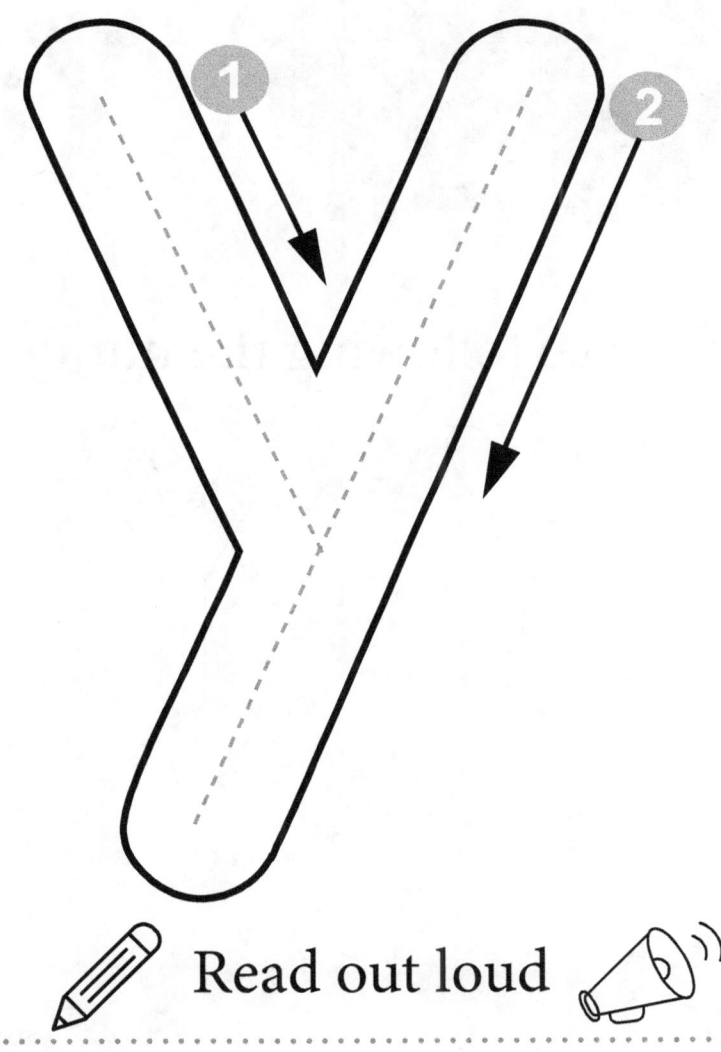

✏️ Read out loud 📣

Yak

 Let's trace following the numbers

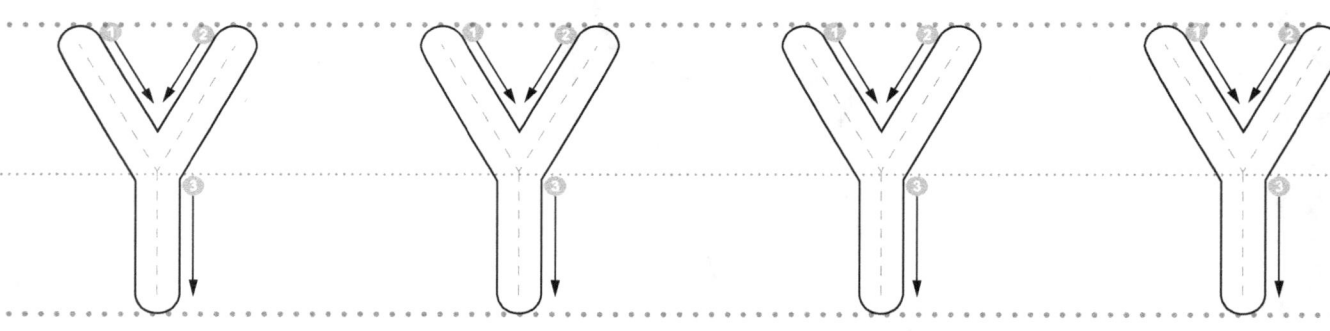

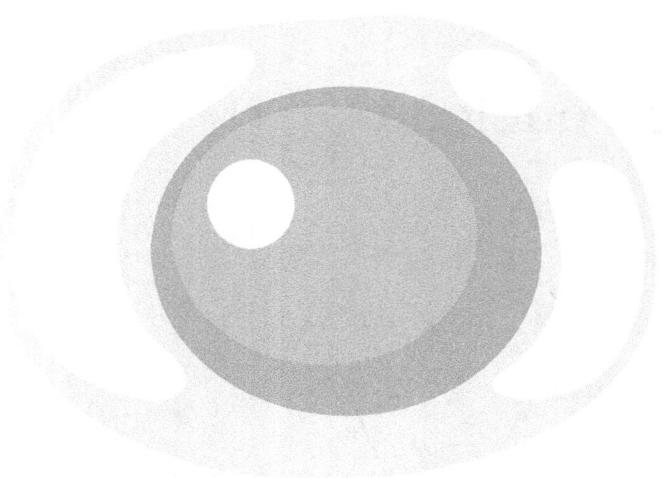

York

yacht

 Read out loud

y y y y

yoga

Find every Y and color them

Trace the dotted line and read out loud

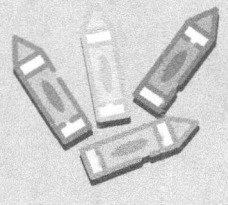 Find every Y and color the sections

Peachidu

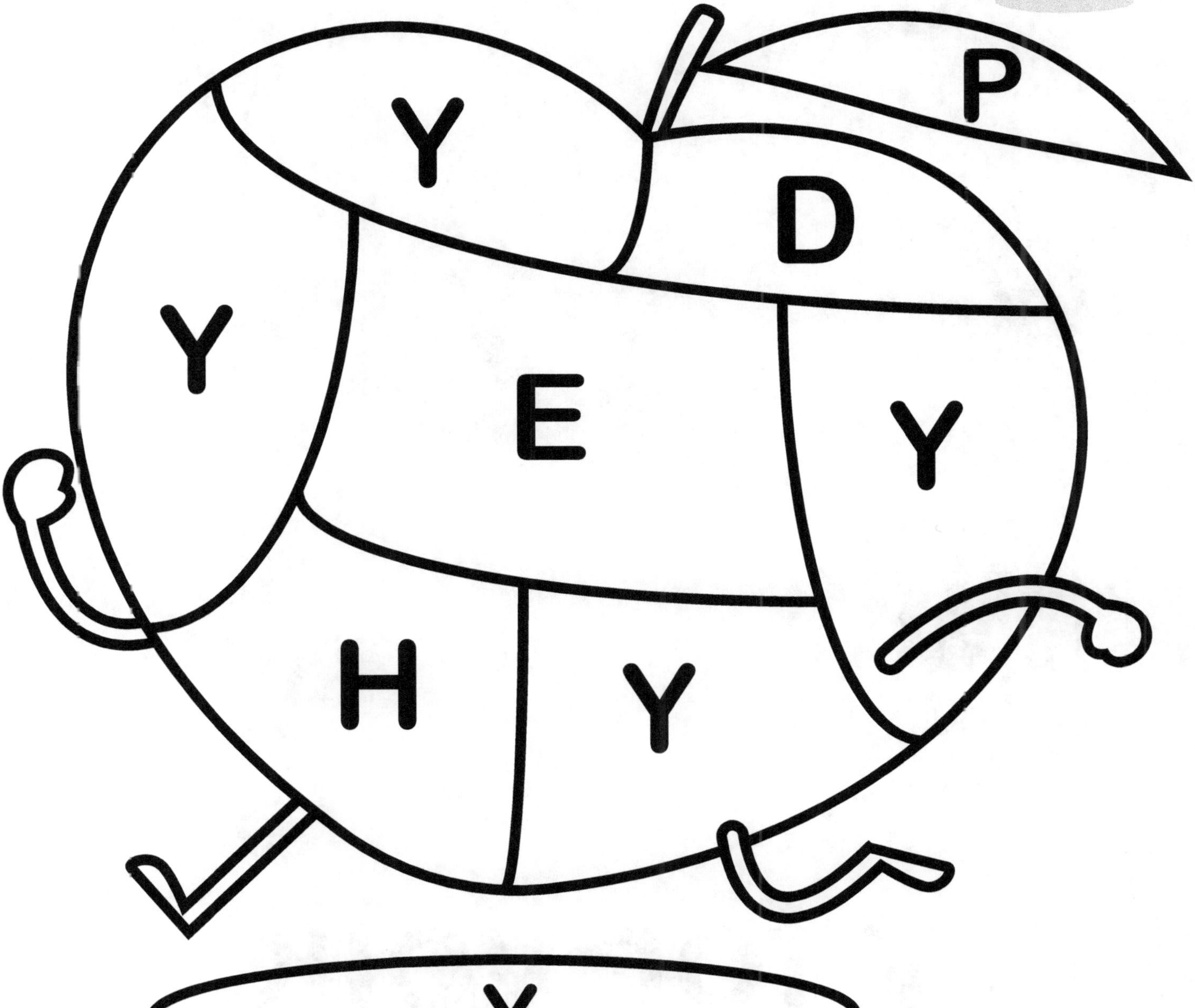

Find every y and circle them

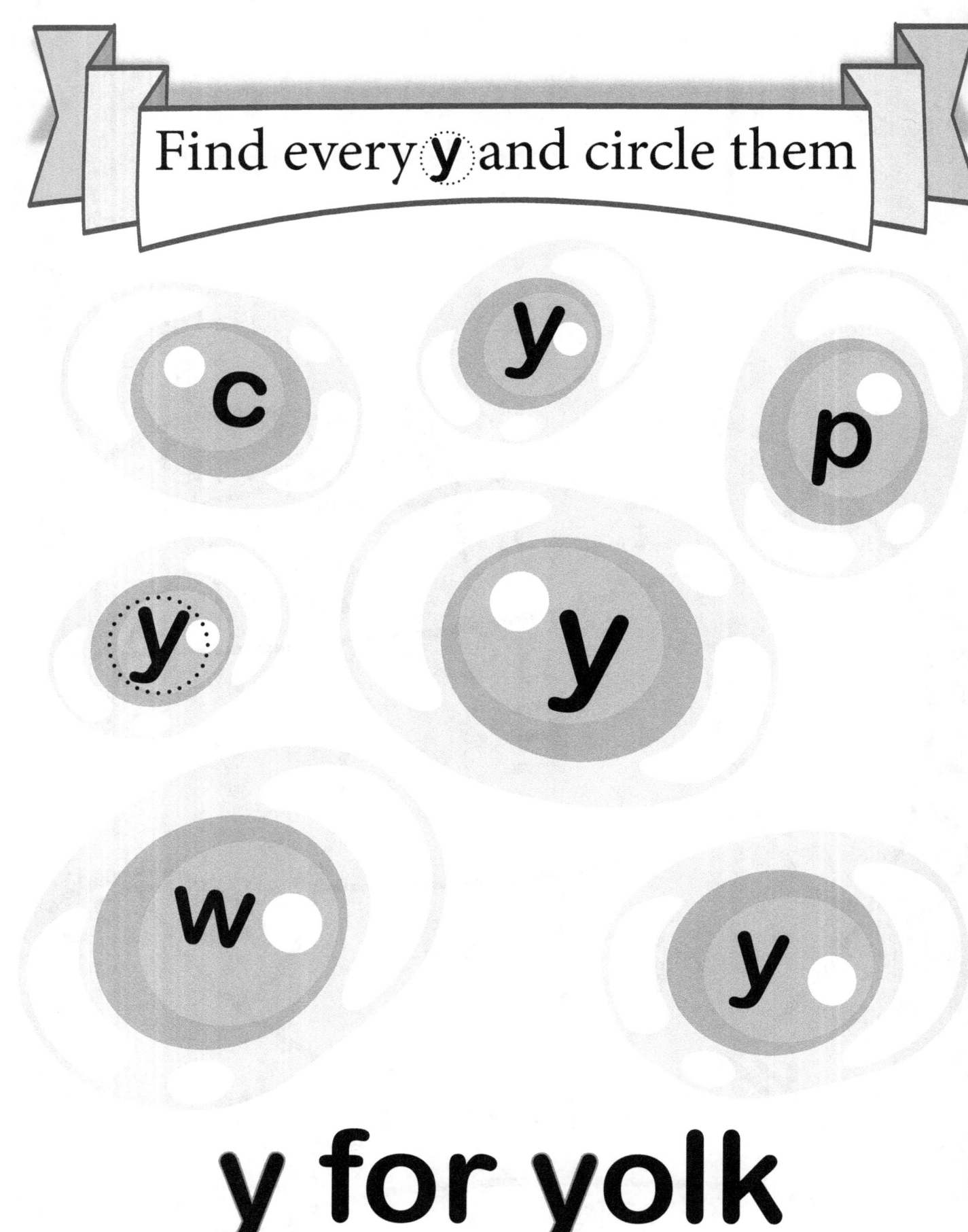

y for yolk

Trace the dotted line and read out loud

Draw lines to match

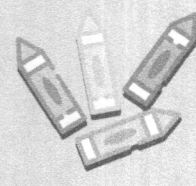 **Find every y and color the sections**

Trace the dotted line and read out loud

Trace the dotted line and read out loud

Find every Y and color them

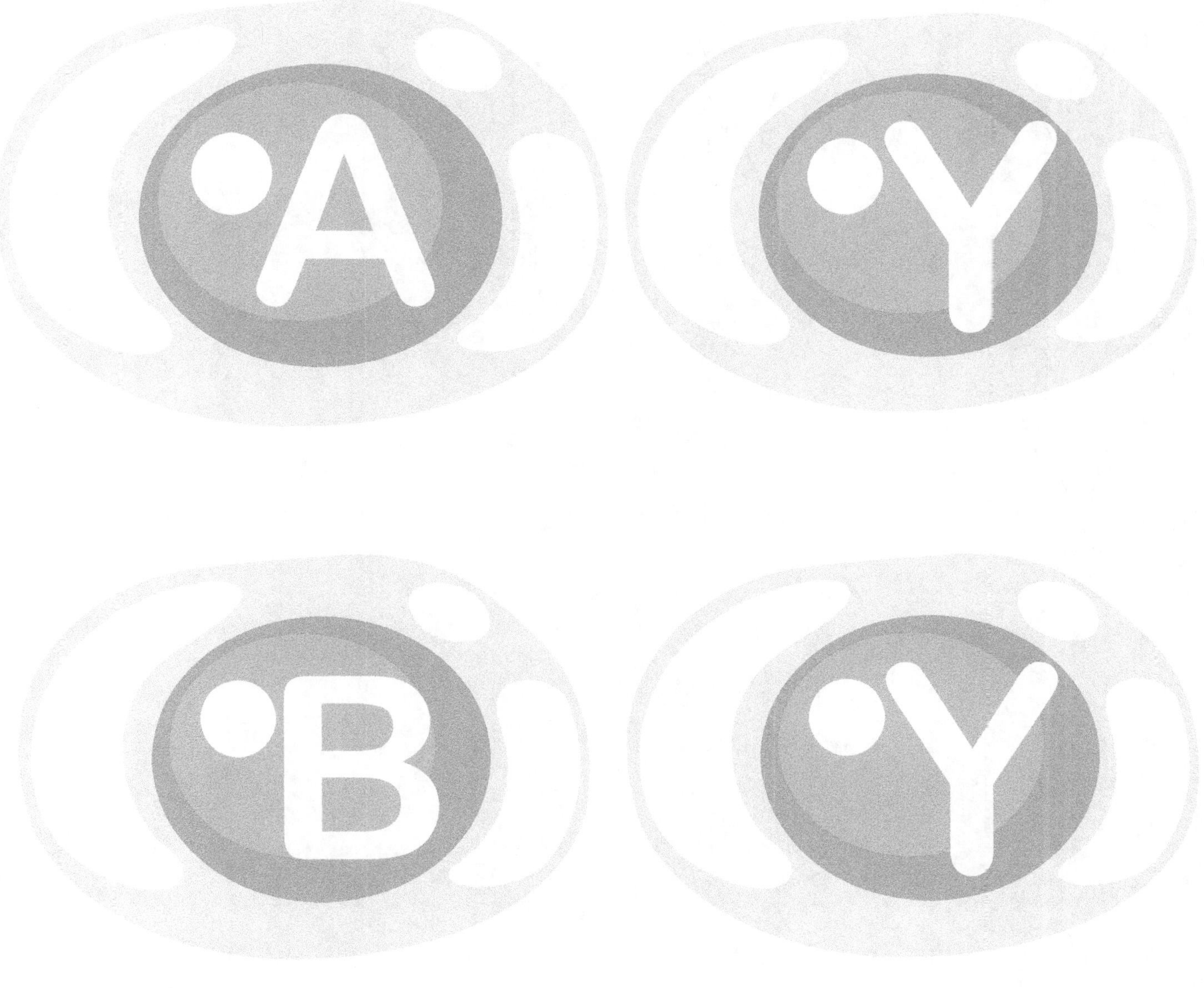

Trace the dotted line and read out loud

 **Find every y and color the sections**

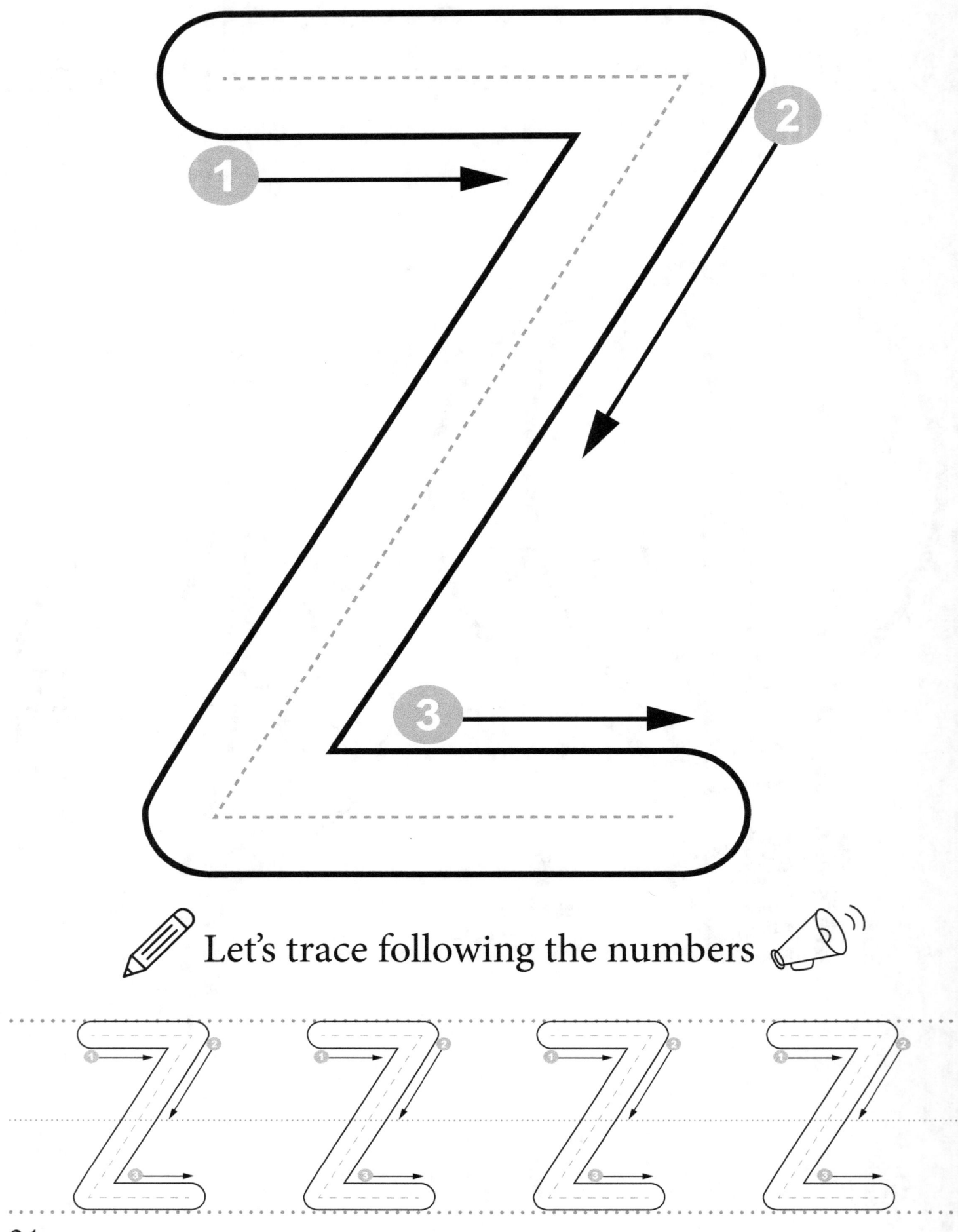

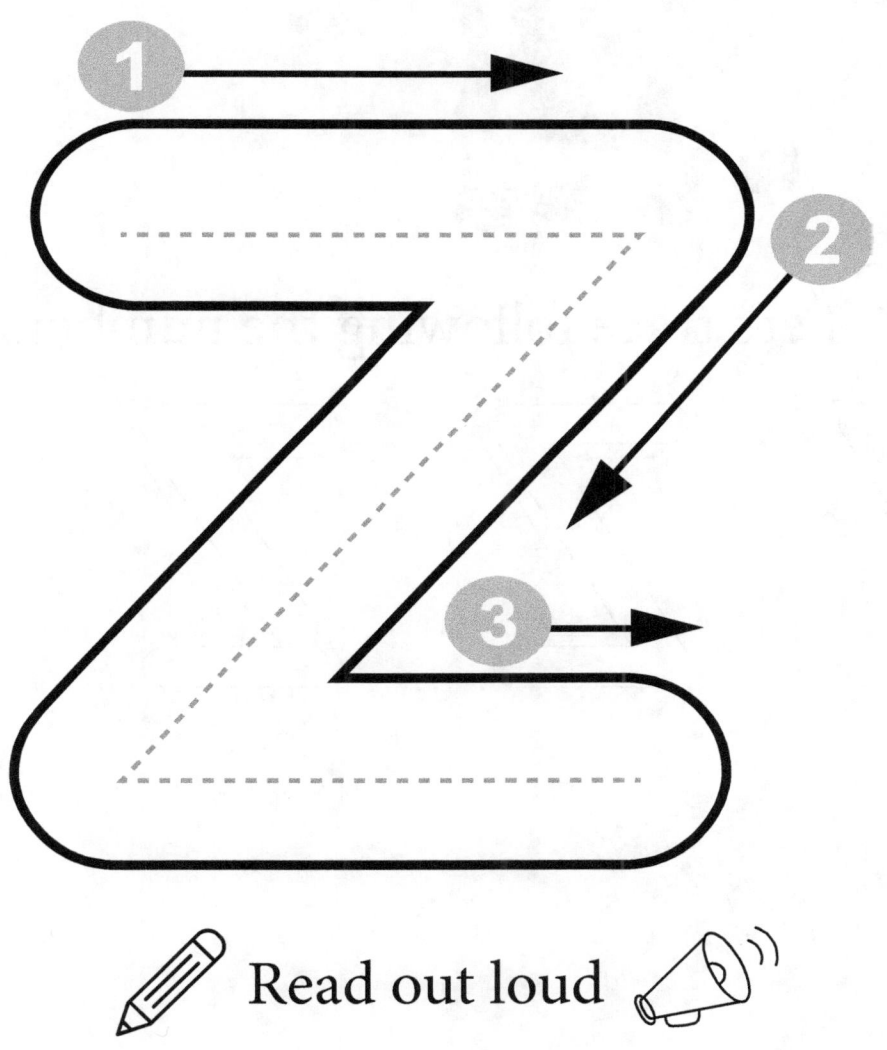

✏️ Read out loud 📢

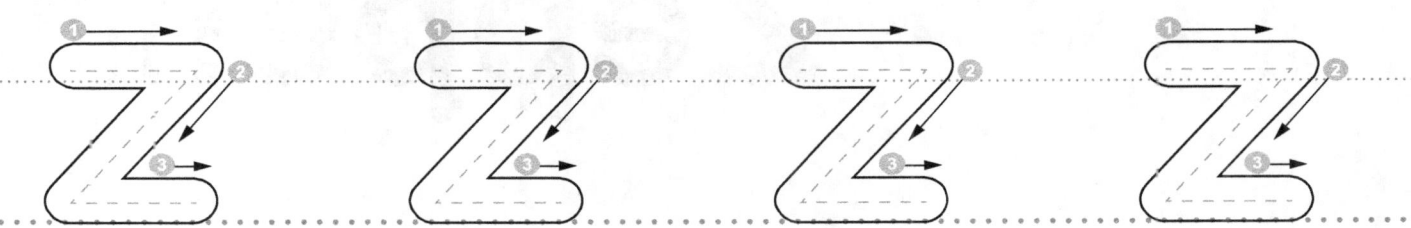

Zebra

✏️ Let's trace following the numbers 📢

Z Z Z Z

Zeppelin

zigzag

 Read out loud

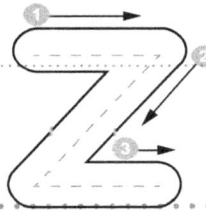 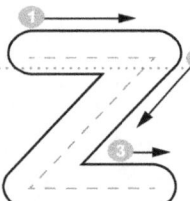 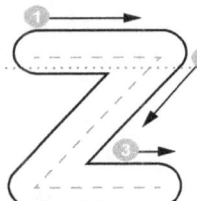 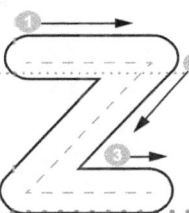

zoo

Find every Z and color them

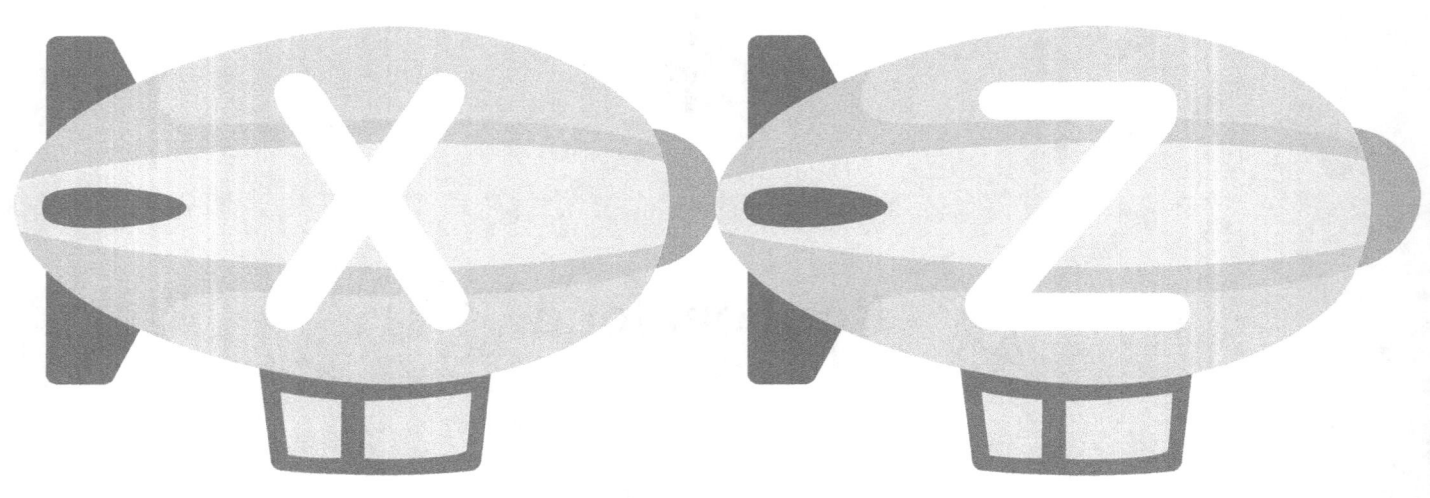

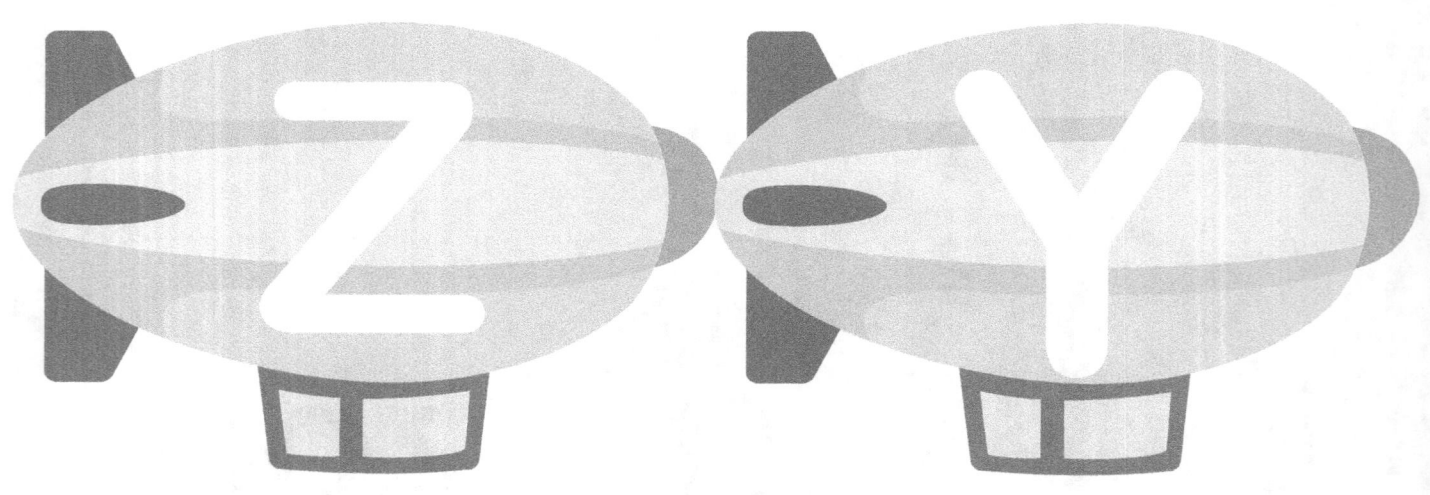

Trace the dotted line and read out loud

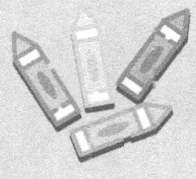# Find every Z and color the sections

Peachidu

Find every z and circle them

z for zigzag

Trace the dotted line and read out loud

Z for Zoo

Draw lines to match

 **Find every z and color the sections**

Trace the dotted line and read out loud

Trace the dotted line and read out loud

Find every Z and color them

Trace the dotted line and read out loud

 **Find every z and color the sections**

Where is Peachidu?

Find and circle!

Let's express your

I am cool

I am hungry

I am playful

I am proud

I am okay

feelings with Peachidu!

Let's express your

I am sad

I am calm

I am rushing

I am frustrated

I am angry

feelings with Peachidu!

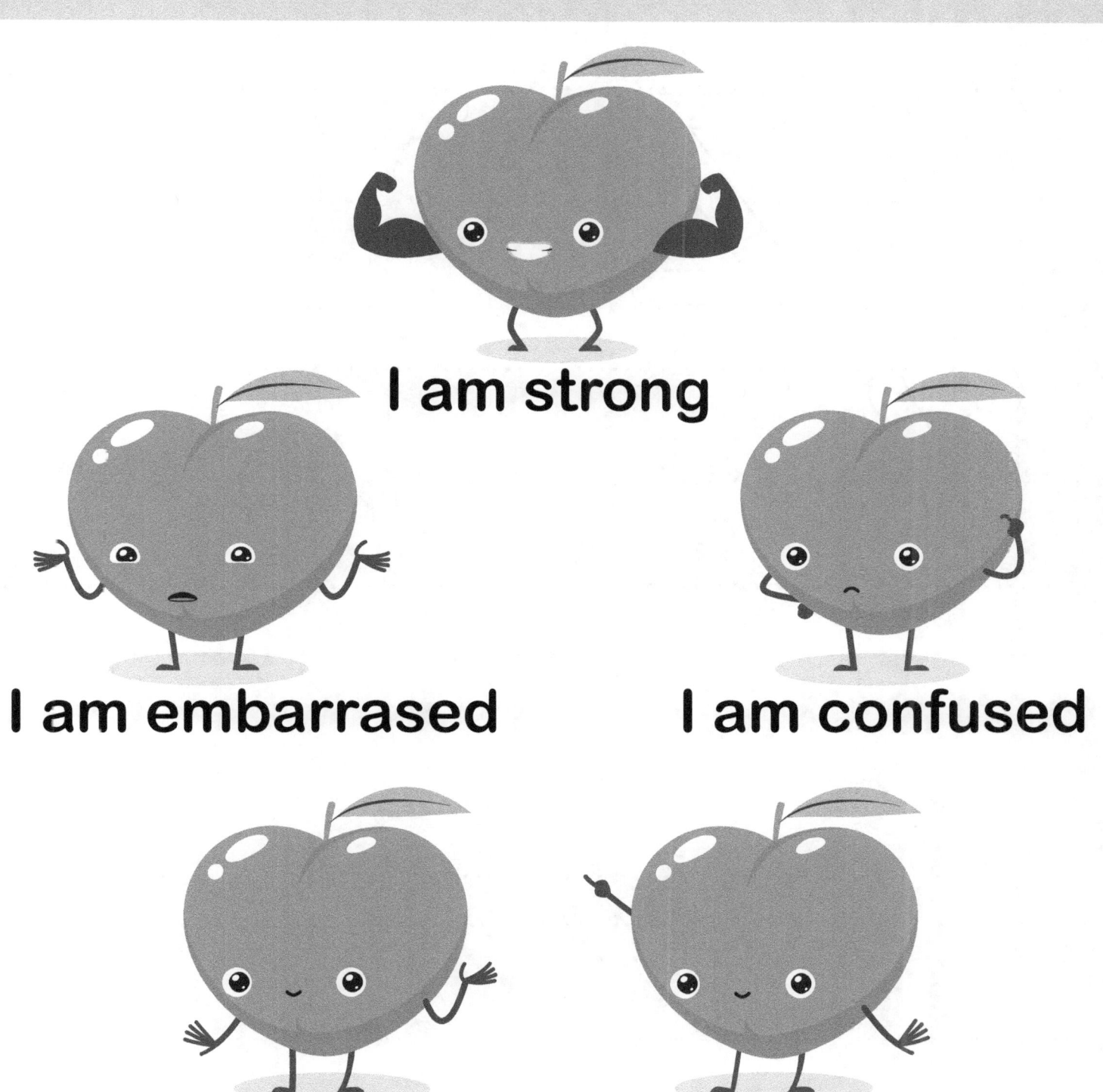

I am strong

I am embarrased

I am confused

I am shy

I am brave

Write YZ and read out loud

Write yz and read out loud

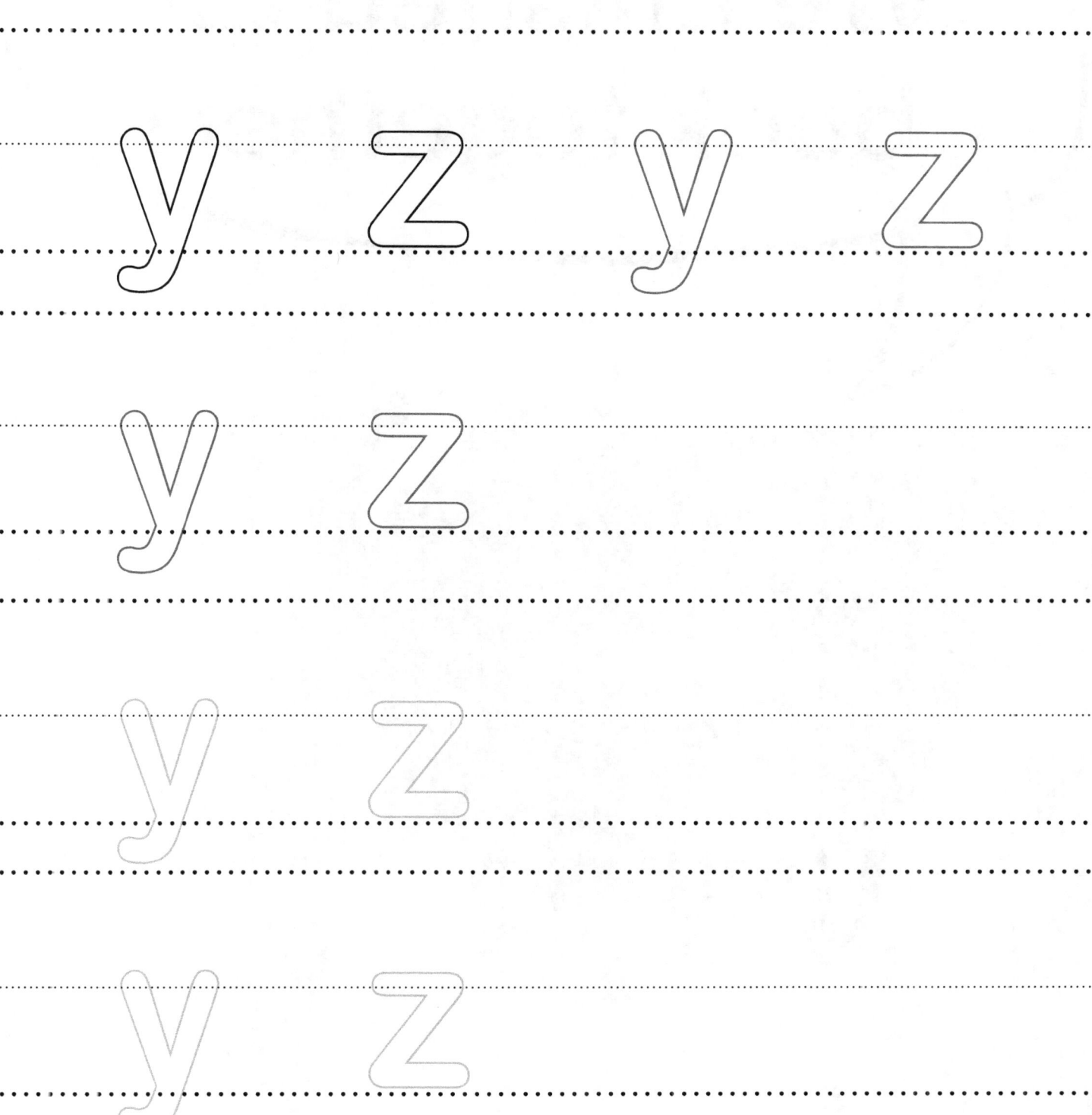

Award

You are amazing!

This award is for

_____ _____
(first name)   (last name)

Great job finishing the book!

Date: _____

Visit Our Website

BigSailorEdu.com

and Get Free & Fun

Educational Material

ABC Workbook Series by Big Sailor Edu

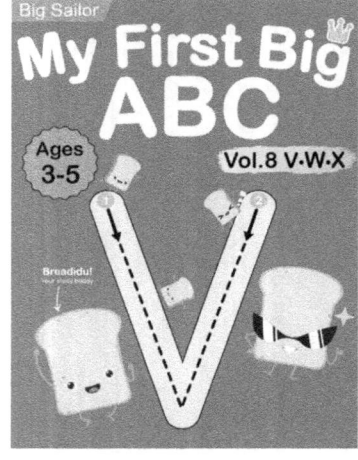

Cambridge Dynasty Press